TYPE SPECIMEN
Missouri Botanical Garden (MO)

ROSACEAE
Rosa memoryae W.H. Lewis

det. Lewis, W. (MO) 2015
MISSOURI BOTANICAL GARDEN HERBARIUM (MO)

UNITED STATES   [126]

ROSACEAE
Rosa foliolosa Nutt.

det. Walter H. Lewis (MO), 2014

Texas: Wise County

LBJ Grasslands, Unit 60, on right-hand
verge of road, slope in sandy soil (PH
7.0).   910 ft
33°24'31"N 097°30'21"W

Petals white to pale pink becoming
darker pink after collecting
(oxidation?)

08 June 2014
Walter H. Lewis, Memory Elvin-Lewis &
Robert J. O'Kennon 21525
MISSOURI BOTANICAL GARDEN HERBARIUM (MO)

Herbaria

A Guide for Young People

Written and Illustrated by
by Kelly LaFarge

Published by
Missouri Botanical Garden Press
4344 Shaw Blvd., St. Louis, Missouri
63110, U.S.A.
www.mbgpress.org

ISBN: 978-1-935641-21-6
Library of Congress Control Number:
2020915461

Printed in China

Editor: Allison M. Brock
Design and typesetting: Ellen Flesch

To my sons, Spencer and Preston. —K. L.

Table of Contents

Herbaria

What Are Herbaria?

Plants give us oxygen. They make the world a more beautiful place. But do plants need to be alive to be helpful to us? What good is a dead plant?

Believe it or not, dead plants can be as useful to us as living ones. Who discovers the secrets hidden in a dead plant? What do dead plants tell us? Where are dead plants kept?

The place that keeps dead plants is called a **herbarium**. The people who collect and care for the dead plants are called **botanists**.

A herbarium is a museum for dried, pressed plant **specimens**. A dried specimen can be just as good for observation as a live plant. Herbaria store dried plants from around the world in one location. The Museum national d'Histoire naturelle (National Museum of Natural History) herbarium in Paris has eight million plant specimens!

"Look deep into nature, and then you will understand everything better."

—Albert Einstein

"All plants are our brothers and sisters. They talk to us and if we listen, we can hear them."
—American Indian proverb

Herbaria help people and scientists observe how plants are the same and how they are different. The plants become a reference for education, medical research, environmental study, and information exchange between countries. Dead plants have a lot to tell us.

Scientists are able to compare specimens to determine new plants. Or the specimens can provide a real sample of an extinct species. The most important benefit herbaria give us is the understanding of the value plants bring to life.

History

When Did the First Herbarium Start?

After food, the medical value of plants became one of the first reasons humans collected plants.

Luca Ghini, an Italian botanist and teacher, established the first herbarium and botanical garden in 1543 in Pisa, Italy. He realized that drying plants gave him samples for his medical students to look at year-round. They didn't have to wait for a plant's growing season to study certain plants. Soon the practice of growing and drying plants spread to other universities in Europe.

Famous Collectors

Jane Colden

Jane Colden is considered the first female botanist in the United States. Jane was born in 1724 in the newly settled American colonies. Raised on her father's estate along the Hudson River in New York, Jane had a large home area where she could explore plants. Encouraged by her father, Jane wrote to leading botanists in Europe and offered to collect plants for them. The plants of the colonies were new to European botanists, and soon Jane was taking requests for specimens. Jane's work helped satisfy the curiosity about the new territory. Three hundred forty descriptions and drawings by Jane can be found at The British Museum in London.

"There is not a sprig of grass that shoots uninteresting to me."
—Thomas Jefferson

Lewis and Clark

On June 20, 1803, President Thomas Jefferson ordered **Meriwether Lewis**, an infantry captain, and **William Clark**, an ex-army lieutenant, to explore a newly purchased land area for the United States. This area was called the Louisiana Territory. Lewis and Clark traveled into the unexplored land west of the Mississippi to the Pacific coast. They found rivers, mountains, and Native American tribes unknown in the East. They observed, gathered, recorded, and drew newfound plants. Two hundred thirty-nine of these mounted plants still exist even after all these years at the Academy of Natural Sciences in Philadelphia.

Like Jane Colden or Lewis and Clark, will you be the first to discover a new plant species? Many are still waiting to be found.

Inspired by Plants

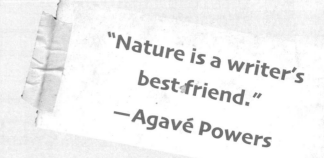
Emily Dickinson

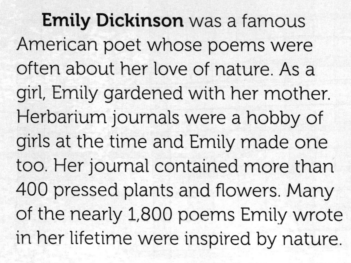

Sometimes the interests we have when we are young become the inspiration for our adult careers.

Emily Dickinson was a famous American poet whose poems were often about her love of nature. As a girl, Emily gardened with her mother. Herbarium journals were a hobby of girls at the time and Emily made one too. Her journal contained more than 400 pressed plants and flowers. Many of the nearly 1,800 poems Emily wrote in her lifetime were inspired by nature.

Today, Emily's herbarium journal is in the Houghton Library at Harvard University in Cambridge, Massachusetts. Maybe you could write a poem about your favorite plant or tree.

Eliot Porter

Eliot Porter spent his childhood summers at his family's vacation home on Great Spruce Head Island, in Penobscot Bay, Maine. Eliot received his first camera at the age of ten. He took pictures of the plants around his vacation home. When Eliot grew up, he started work as a research scientist, but left his job to work as a full-time photographer. His favorite plants to photograph were lichens, a type of algae fungus. In the 1960s he became famous for his artistic use of color film when photographing nature. Porter published over twenty-five books of nature photos, helping to preserve the beauty of nature.

You could draw, paint, or photograph your favorite flower or shrub. Maybe someday plants will be an inspiration for you.

Uses of a Herbarium

What Are Herbaria Used For?

A museum that stores dried plants from all around the world is a valuable **resource** for scientists, teachers, artists, farmers, and ecologists. It is a permanent record of plant life. A herbarium is a source of supply, support, or aid to plants. It's a resource of information available to help anyone curious about plants. Herbaria may have uses we haven't even thought of yet, uses you may need when you are an adult.

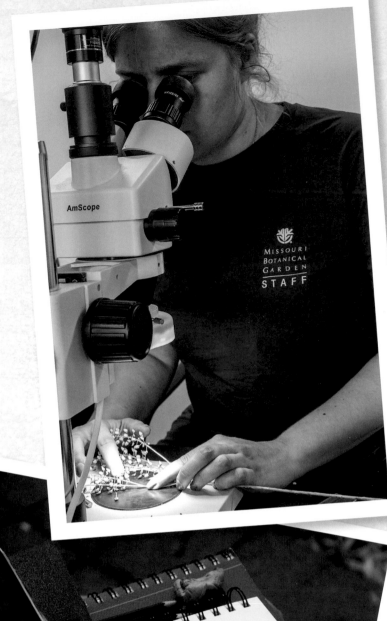

"Nature is my medicine."

—Sara Moss-Wolfe

USES OF A HERBARIUM

Who Uses a Herbarium?

Scientists study the similarities and differences of plant families. They can see changes in the same kinds of plants that grow in different locations. They look for changes in plants caused by pests, pollution, or evolution.

- **Medical researchers** can use small samples of plants to invent new medicines.

- **Teachers** come to the herbarium to be trained to teach their students about **botany** or forestry.

- **Artists** observe plant specimens to aid themselves with illustrating or painting.

- **Law enforcement investigators** receive help identifying plant particles found at a crime scene.

- **Farmers** identify weeds that hurt their crops or look for better kinds of plants to grow.

- **Ecologists** may be able to discover the mysteries of why some plants have become extinct. And maybe they can discover ways to make sure all our plants don't become extinct.

Can you think of other professions that may need a herbarium? How could you, a student, use a herbarium?

Collecting Plants

How Are Plants Collected?

Herbaria need a lot of plants. They need people to collect them. The people who travel to prairies, forests, or deserts to look for specimens are called **field collectors**. Field collectors are people who love to travel, love plants, and care about helping the Earth. It can be a difficult job but doing it successfully gives them satisfaction and sometimes recognition. If you are a collector who finds a specimen that has never been discovered, you could become famous. You might even have your name as part of the new plant's name.

THE NEWS

Student Discovers New Species

Bobby Jones from St. Louis, Missouri, is being credited with discovering a new plant species. When asked how he managed to find what no other scientist had, he replied, "I spend a lot of time outdoors. I got a magnifying glass for my birthday. I love to look at all kinds of plants with it. When I found one I really liked, I tried to find it on the internet. I couldn't find it. So, Mom took me to the herbarium. A botanist there said, 'Congratulations. You've discovered a new species.' Wow, I was just doing what I love to do—look at plants!"

To collect for a herbarium, the most important thing a field collector does is document and write down everything they see, do, and take. A **field journal** is essential. A field journal can be a notebook, tablet, or computer. When collectors find a plant, this is what they record:

Date: _____

Location/Country: _____

County: _____ State: _____

Latitude: _____ Town: _____

Habitat: _____ Longitude: _____

What else is growing nearby? _____
_____

Observations: Is it a shrub? A tree? How tall is it?

Does it smell? Does it have a good fragrance?

What does it feel like? sticky, prickly, soft

Where Are Plants Collected?

Plants grow nearly everywhere on Earth, so collectors go everywhere. Field collectors may hike miles across the parched deserts of Africa, climb the frosty Himalayan Mountains, or wade in the snake-filled swamps of Borneo. They have to go. They are looking for the secrets hidden in plants.

If you were a field collector, where would you be willing to go?

Monitoring climate change in Nepal

Crossing makeshift bridges in Bolivia

Collecting plants in Costa Rica

"Those who dwell, as scientists or laymen, among the beauties and mysteries of the earth are never alone or weary of life."

—Rachel Carson

Climbing trees in Peru

Scaling mountains in Tibet

15

How Are Plant Specimens Sent to the Herbarium?

Field collectors work hard to collect plant specimens. Then they need to make sure the plants make it safely back to the herbarium.

Their plants need to go in a **plant press**. What does a plant press do? It removes the water from the plants and helps them dry flat. The press is stacked, like a sandwich, with layers of cardboard, absorbent paper, folded newspaper with the plant inside, more cardboard, more absorbent paper, another plant inside newspaper, and so on. Collectors can stack and press many specimens together. In five to seven days their plants should be flat and dry. A dried plant will last for hundreds of years. The Botanical Research Institute of Texas in Fort Worth has a specimen dating back to 1791. Although it was found in what is today the state of Texas, it was discovered when the area was known as Mexico!

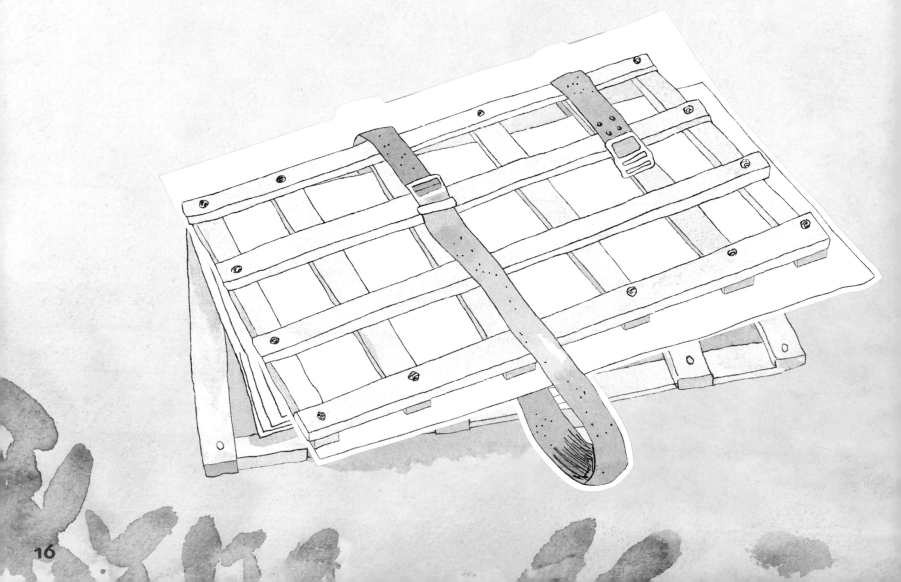

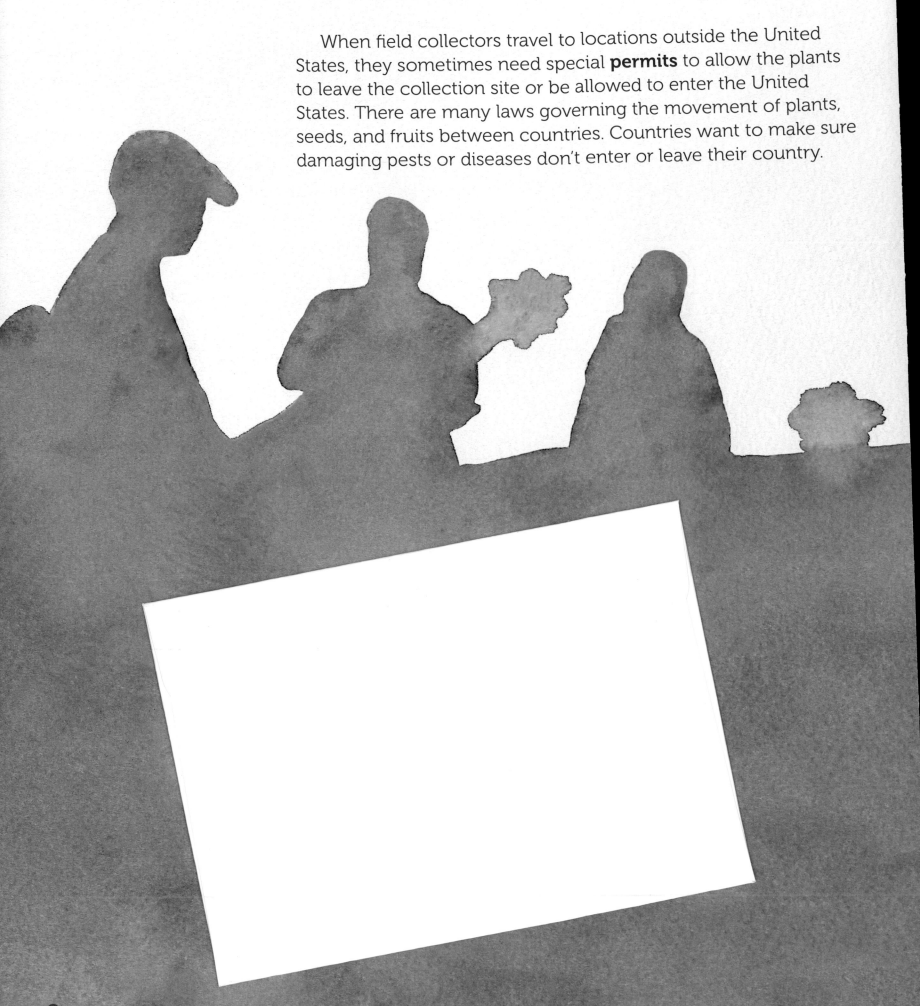

When field collectors travel to locations outside the United States, they sometimes need special **permits** to allow the plants to leave the collection site or be allowed to enter the United States. There are many laws governing the movement of plants, seeds, and fruits between countries. Countries want to make sure damaging pests or diseases don't enter or leave their country.

Preservation

How Are Plants Preserved at the Herbarium?

Botanists are always excited to have new plants arrive at the herbarium. Unpacking presses is as thrilling as opening a gift.

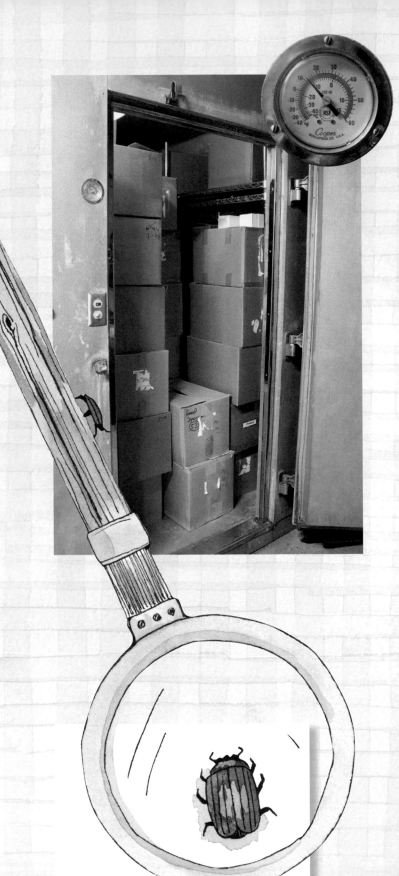

Sometimes plants are sent so fast to the herbarium that they are still damp.

To help further dry the plants, the presses are placed into a **drying cabinet**. This special cabinet blows 100° Fahrenheit air around the presses.

Could you survive for very long at the temperature of −40° Fahrenheit? No, and hopefully bugs can't either. Sometimes bugs and diseases travel along with the plant specimens. These things can eat cabinets full of herbarium specimens. As soon as the plants come out of the dryer they are immediately placed in a freezer at −40° Fahrenheit for four days. This kills any unwanted pests and keeps them from entering and harming other herbarium specimens.

Herbarium Beetle

Adult beetles are 2–3 mm in length and live only three to four weeks, but they can chew cabinets full of specimens.

Acharagma roseana

Hello, Cousin!

Hello, Cousin!

Acharagma roseanum

Scientists and visitors love to come and look at the plants that have been **preserved**. But how can botanists make it easy to organize, view, and protect delicate specimens all at the same time? They type unique labels and barcodes, and mount the plants on special paper.

The first thing a botanist does when she opens up a plant press is to correctly identify the plant and find its proper name. She may look in plant books, read data from other herbaria, or ask other botanists. She types a label that has the plant's scientific name. All plants have a two-part name, **genus** and **species**, written in Latin. The first part of a plant's name is like your family's last name. All plants in the same genus are given the same first name. But all plants in a genus are not exactly alike. The genera are divided into smaller groups called species, like your first name. In plants, it's last name, then first name. These two names together are a plant's scientific botanical name.

Some herbaria today are attaching barcodes along with identification labels. They look just like the barcodes on products at a grocery store. When a computer scans the specimen's barcode, even more information is available. You may be able to see photos of the plant's **habitat**, location maps, measurements of the live specimen, and notes of the field collector's experience.

PLANTS OF COLORADO

DNA VOUCHER

CHENOPDIACEAE

Sarcobatus vermiculatus (Hook.) Torr. Dupl. det. M. Piep 2005

COLORADO: Gunnison County. About 16 mi. east of Montrose, at junction of US Hwy 50 and Colorado Hwy 347. Coord: 38° 29'17" N, 107° 44'19" W, elev. ca. 7561 ft.

Common shrubs to ca. 2 m tall. Silica gel dried leaves preserved at the DNA Bank, Missouri Botanical Garden.

Robert Merrill King and
Robert M. Garvey No. 13891   July 12, 2005

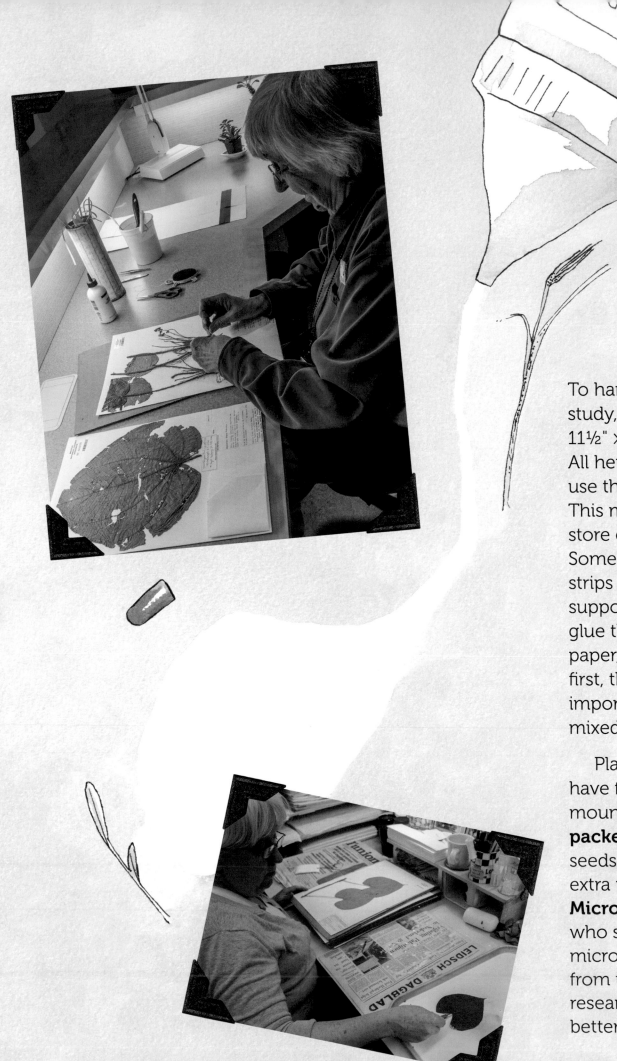

To handle specimens to study, they must be glued on 11½" × 16½" **mounting paper**. All herbaria around the world use the exact same sized paper. This makes it easy to trade and store exchanged specimens. Some bulky plants need small strips of strapping tape for extra support. Mounters, people who glue the plants on the mounting paper, always glue the labels first, then the plant. This is important so plants don't get mixed up.

Plant specimens may also have fragment packets on the mounting paper. **Fragment packets** contain extra bark, seeds, buds, or any other extra pieces from the plant. **Microbiologists**, people who study life forms at the microscopic level, use samples from the fragment packets. Their research of plants can lead to better foods and new medicines.

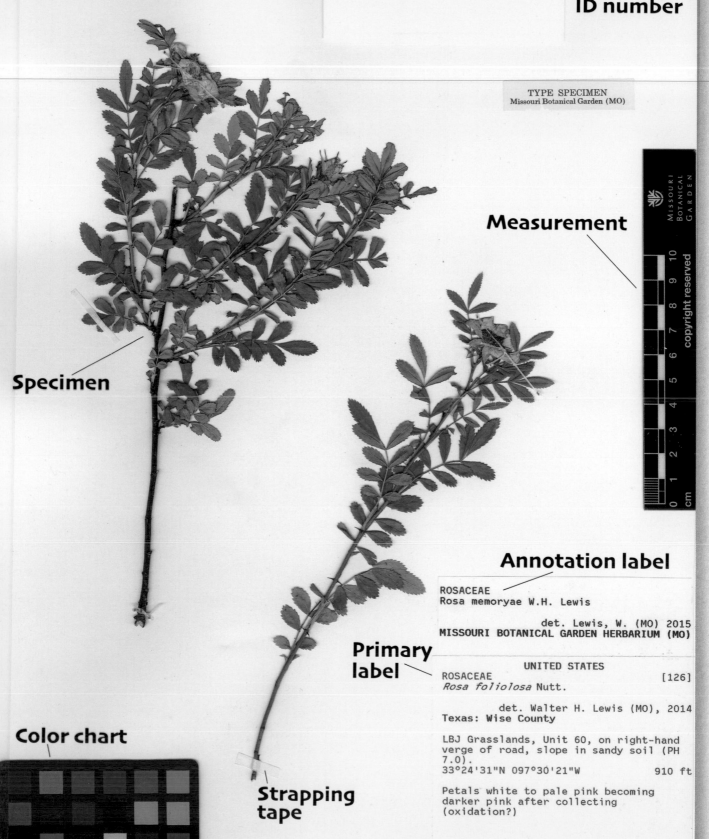

Mounting paper

Fragment packet

N° 6583699

ID number

TYPE SPECIMEN
Missouri Botanical Garden (MO)

Measurement

MISSOURI
BOTANICAL
GARDEN

copyright reserved

10
9
8
7
6
5
4
3
2
1
0
cm

Specimen

Annotation label

ROSACEAE
Rosa memoryae W.H. Lewis

det. Lewis, W. (MO) 2015
MISSOURI BOTANICAL GARDEN HERBARIUM (MO)

Primary label

UNITED STATES
ROSACEAE   [126]
Rosa foliolosa Nutt.

det. Walter H. Lewis (MO), 2014
Texas: Wise County

LBJ Grasslands, Unit 60, on right-hand
verge of road, slope in sandy soil (PH
7.0).
33°24'31"N 097°30'21"W   910 ft

Petals white to pale pink becoming
darker pink after collecting
(oxidation?)

Color chart

**Strapping
tape**

08 June 2014
Walter H. Lewis, Memory Elvin-Lewis &
Robert J. O'Kennon 21525
MISSOURI BOTANICAL GARDEN HERBARIUM (MO)

23

Offering seeds for observation is another service of a herbarium. But what do botanists do when they have a giant double-coconut seed, the world's biggest seed? They can weigh up to 44 pounds. How would it fit on mounting paper? Botanists store these large specimens in special cabinets called **carpological files**.

"The creation of a thousand forests is in one acorn."

—Ralph Waldo Emerson

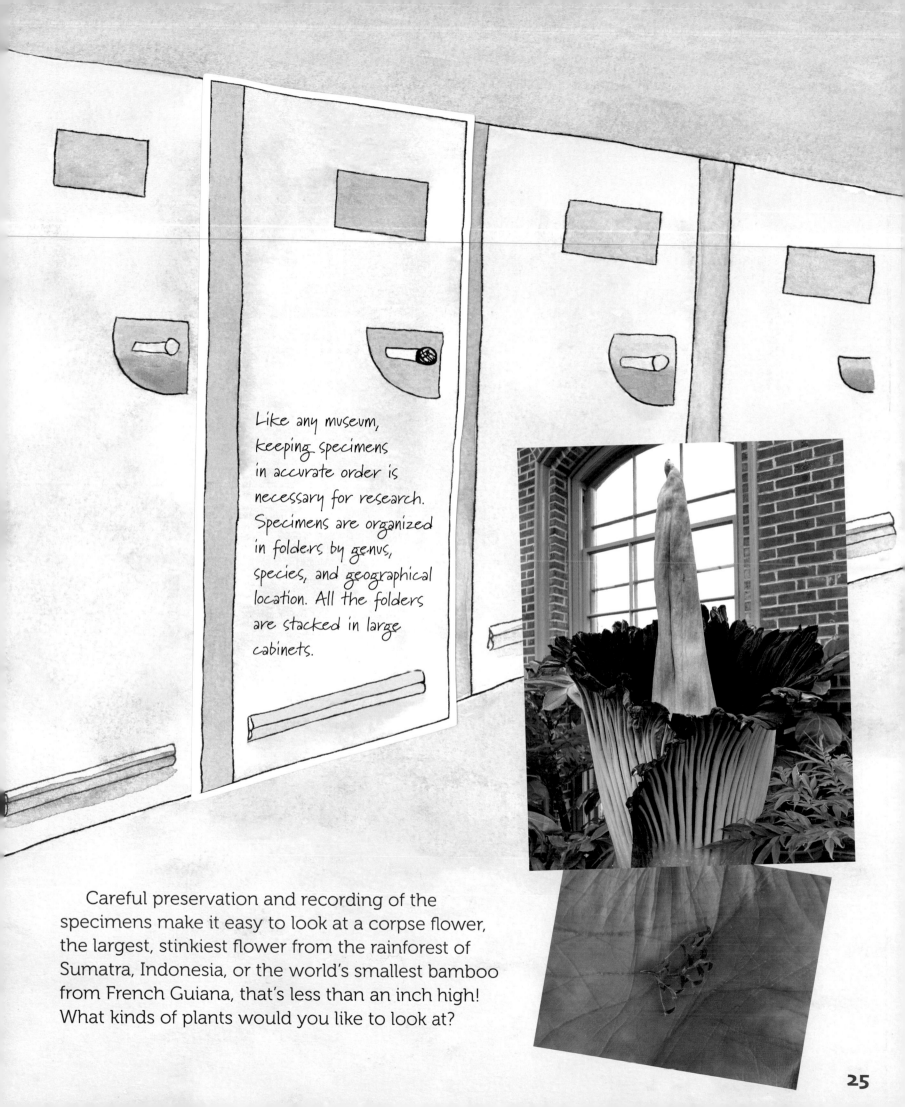

Like any museum, keeping specimens in accurate order is necessary for research. Specimens are organized in folders by genus, species, and geographical location. All the folders are stacked in large cabinets.

Careful preservation and recording of the specimens make it easy to look at a corpse flower, the largest, stinkiest flower from the rainforest of Sumatra, Indonesia, or the world's smallest bamboo from French Guiana, that's less than an inch high! What kinds of plants would you like to look at?

Herbarium Benefits

Who Benefits from Herbaria?

A herbarium is a museum for dried, pressed plant specimens. It's a place for innovation, exploration, and inspiration. It's a scientific laboratory where curious people can research answers to important questions about our life on Earth.

We are still making discoveries about our planet. There will be uses for herbaria we haven't even thought of yet. Will you be the doctor that researches the plant that provides the miracle cure for an illness? Will you be the farmer that grows the hardiest plants to feed starving people? Will you be the field collector that finds the plant that adds to our understanding of the mysteries of life? People and animals depend on plants.

Herbarium Locations

Where Are Herbaria?

There are herbarium museums on almost every continent in the world. The largest herbarium is the Museum national d'Histoire naturelle in Paris, France. They have eight million plant specimens. The Komarov Botanical Institute in St. Petersburg, Russia, has six million plants. The Royal Botanic Gardens in Kew, England, has seven million plant specimens.

In the United States, the New York Botanical Garden has more than seven million specimens. The Missouri Botanical Garden has nearly seven million specimens. Other large collections may be found at the Harvard University Herbaria in Cambridge, Massachusetts, the United States National Herbarium at the Smithsonian Institution in Washington D.C., and the Field Museum in Chicago, Illinois.

Greetings from FRANCE

Greetings from KEW GARDENS LONDON

"One touch of nature makes the whole world kin."
—William Shakespeare

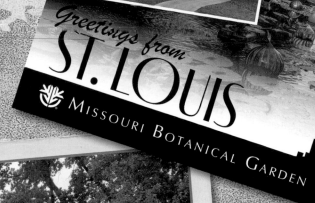

Greetings from
ST. LOUIS
Missouri Botanical Garden

GREETINGS FROM
RUSSIA
St. Petersburg
KOMAROV BOTANICAL INSTITUTE

GREETINGS FROM
NEW YORK
NEW YORK BOTANICAL GARDEN

Herbarium Facts

There are almost 400,000 species of plants on Earth.

Floristic botanists study a particular geographic region and all of its plant species.

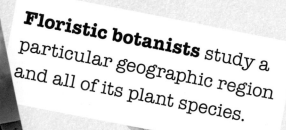

In the United States, one in twenty plants has yet to be discovered.

Corn, wheat, and rice are half of the food consumed by humans worldwide.

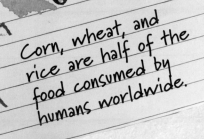

The Royal Botanic Gardens in Kew, London, has more than two billion seeds saved in its Millennium Seed Bank.

An ideal plant specimen includes samples of flowers, fruits, and leaves.

PVLMONARIA fo-
calycibus brevissimis pro- ... lus ovatis glabris, scapo laxo,
limbo campanifor- mi quinquepartito

Monographic botanists study a particular group of plants regardless of where they grow.

Scientists estimate that 50,000 species of plants, one in six, are still waiting to be discovered.

paleobotany | noun
pa·leo·bot·a·ny |
pey-lee-oh-bot-n-ee
The study of plant fossils.

Flowering plants are the largest plant group in the world.

systematics | noun
sys·tem·at·ics
The difficult work of identifying and organizing plant specimens.

Glossary

botanist: a scientist who studies plant life.

botany: the science of plant life.

carpological file: cabinets or drawers used to store larger parts of plant specimens such as seeds, bark, or buds.

Colden, Jane (1724–1766): considered to be the first female botanist in the United States.

Dickinson, Emily (1830–1886): famous American poet; wrote nature-inspired poetry.

drying cabinet: warm air cabinet used to dry plants still in presses.

field collector: scientist, researcher, or hobbyist who collects plant specimens.

field journal: notebook, tablet, or computer used by field collectors to record data about plants and their habitats.

fragment packet: small envelope on mounting paper containing extra pieces from a plant specimen.

genus: a group that has common characteristics.

Ghini, Luca (1490–1556): Italian botanist; created first botanical garden and herbarium.

habitat: the location, conditions, and weather surrounding a living thing.

herbarium: a collection of dried plant specimens mounted and arranged for research; herbaria is the plural form.

Lewis and Clark: leaders appointed by President Jefferson to explore the Louisiana Purchase (1800s); first to write observations of plants in the territory.

microbiologists: people who study microscopic forms of life.

mounting paper: 11½" × 16½" acid-free paper used to mount plant specimens; same size used all over the world.

permit: official forms, letters, or papers that allow specimens to travel between countries.

plant press: a wooden frame with layers of paper and cardboard designed to press water out of plants and dry them flat.

Porter, Eliot (1901–1990): nature-inspired photographer; used color film technology for nature studies.

preserve: to keep safe, intact, or free from decay.

resource: a source of supply, support, or aid that is available when needed.

species: organisms very closely related.

specimen: an item used for testing, examination, or study.

Acknowledgments

A very sincere thank you to the Botanic Research Institute of Texas (BRIT) for allowing the child in me to explore and learn the fascinating process of herbarium science.

Gratitude to: Mr. Barney Lipscomb, Leonhardt Chair of Texas Botany, Head of Publications.

Photo and Illustrations Credits

All illustrations by Kelly LaFarge. **title page**, Missouri Botanical Garden; **front cover**, top Kat Niehaus, bottom Tom Incrocci; **4**, Benh Lieu Song; **6**, Stephanie Keil; **7**, Museo Botanico, Sistema Museale di Ateneo, Università di Pisa; **9**, top Archives & Special Collections at Amherst College, bottom Amon Carter Museum of American Art, Fort Worth, Texas; **10**, top Cassidy Moody, left Rainer Bussmann, right Claire Cohen; **11**, top Jill Setlich, middle Rodolfo Vásquez, bottom Maddy Gordon; **12**, Allison Brock; **14**, left Elsa Hart, right Alfredo Fuentes, bottom Maria Marta Chavarría; **15**, background Rodolfo Vásquez, bottom Missouri Botanical Garden staff; **18**, permit courtesy of John Atwood with permission from Missouri State Parks; **19**, top and middle Stephanie Keil, bottom Sheridan Hentrich; **20**, Stephanie Keil; **22**, top Dan Brown, bottom Maddy Gordon; **23**, Missouri Botanical Garden; **24**, Stephanie Keil; **25**, top Stephanie Keil, middle Sundos Schneider, bottom Smithsonian Institution; **26**, left Mary Lou Olson, right Trenton Almgren-Davis; **28**, top Benh Lieu Song, bottom © RBG Kew, Roman Fox, Sabrina Mazzeo, Jurica Koletić, Manuele Sangalli, Dominika Gregušova, Samuel Wolfl; **29**, top Steve Frank, Kent Burgess, middle Alexey Sergeev, bottom Marlon Co Photography; **30–31**, Missouri Botanical Garden Press.

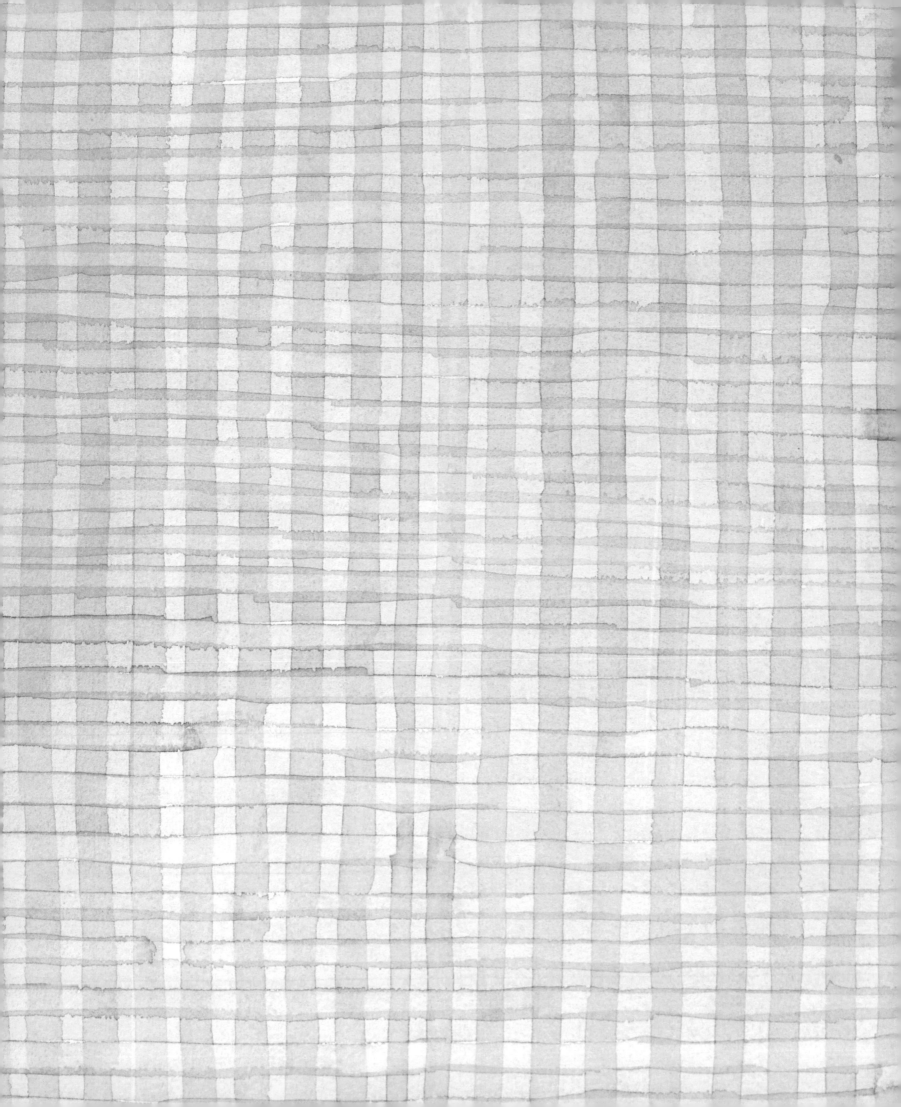